THE
FAST
GUIDE
TO
ARCHITECTURAL
FORM

#thefastguidetoarchitecturalform

BIS Publishers
Building Het Sieraad
Postjesweg 1
1057 DT Amsterdam
The Netherlands

T +31 (0)20 515 02 30
F +31 (0)20 515 02 39
bis@bispublishers.com
www.bispublishers.com

ISBN 978 90 6369 411 1

THE FAST GUIDE TO ARCHITECTURAL FORM

Baires Raffaelli

Translated by Silvia Antonini

BISPUBLISHERS

FOREWORD BY LUIGI PRESTINENZA PUGLISI

You can read this book in two different ways: like a textbook or like a challenge. As a textbook it's precious, since there are not many clever books to teach the new—and not so new—strategies of shape-composition. But as a textbook, it is destined to become outdated and to be contradicted. There is not one talented designer who fails to make every precept useless and obsolete—the wisest and most reasonable above all. That's why it's better to view this book as a challenge, as a move in an endless chess game against the eternal, but changeable, laws of creativity.

"What I am going to tell you about is what we teach our physics students in the third or fourth year of graduate school... It is my task to convince you not to turn away because you don't understand it. You see my physics students don't understand it... That is because I don't understand it. Nobody does."

Richard Feynman

INTRODUCTION

Architecture is born of an idea, and the idea is a specific mental structure we use to organize, understand and give a meaning to experiences and outside information. That's why 'good planning solutions are not interesting for their physical results alone, but most of all for the ideas that lead them'.

Architecture fails and becomes mere planning without the guidance of matrix ideas being the foundation of the design of spaces and buildings. You can afterwards enrich design with decorations or formal solutions, but this will not turn it into "Architecture", it will only be formalism at best, since 'Architecture lives in a building's DNA, in a deep-rooted sensitivity that permeates the whole structure'.

One can think of an architectural shape as a 'volume' existing in 'space' or, on the contrary, as 'space'—delimited and contained—'Space that presses and that endures pressure'.

What we mean to investigate here is the relationship between the choice of a particular 'shape-container' and the further formal actions taken on its volume, studying, case by case, how they depend on each other. Once the perceptual choice of the shape has been made (or fixed), we want to examine the following planning actions that contribute to functional, distributive, and technical solutions, without betraying the original choice, and, if possible, enhancing it.

DEFINITION OF THE SHAPE

"By "form" is meant the visual appearance of a building (line, outline, shape, composition); by "function" the structural and functional requirements of a building (construction, shelter, program, organization, use, occupancy, materials, social purpose). Form of course can be said to have a metaphysical "function" to represent or express an idea, but that sense of the word is not used here."

Peter Eisenman

Studio Fuksas, *Church San Paolo Apostolo*, Foligno.
photo by © Giorgio Panacci

"Two different concepts of Architecture face each other nowadays. One looking for dematerialization, transparence and the "so called" flows. The other is bulkier, made of body, substance, matter and mass."

Luigi Prestinenza Puglisi

A SEEMINGLY FULL VOLUME

YOU CAN

Puncture the surface with holes—many if you like—but only if small when compared to the total mass.
Remove mass, feigning discovery of a full space by showing great thickness.

YOU CAN'T

Apply punctures that are big when compared to the total mass.
Remove mass and expose the real thickness of the shell.

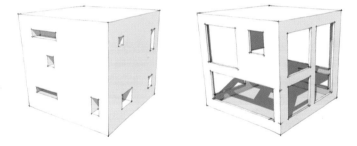

KEEP IN MIND

Puncture the surface with holes—many if you like—but only if small when compared to the total mass.

Keep the ratio of filled–to–removed parts (or curtain - wall –to – punctures) always in favour of full surfaces.

Handle punctures like they were removed parts of the full volume, giving prominence to the thickness of the feigned matter. Try not to stress the surfaces that necessarily define the shell.

#thefastguidetoarchitecturalform

MASS AND MATTER

#massmatter

Emmanuelle Moureaux, *Sugamo Shinkin Bank*, Tokyo, Japan.
photo by Daisuke Shima / Nacása & Partners

MVRDV, *Double House*, Utrecht, Netherlands.
photo by Christian Richters

"The heterogeneous landscape of contemporary design seems to express a sort of "superficial" complexity where the trend to bidimensional conceptualization is certainly a defensive response to the current conditions of architectural production"

Giovanni Corbellini

A SEEMINGLY–EMPTY–WITHIN VOLUME, DEFINED BY A SINGLE CONTINUOUS SURFACE

YOU CAN

Apply big punctures.
Let the shell show its bulk.
Puncture corners.

YOU CAN'T

Make it look like an 'excavation'.
Give prominence to corner continuity.

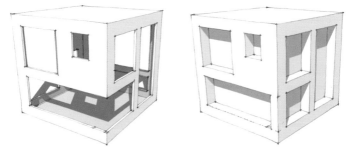

KEEP IN MIND

Keep the ratio of filled–to–removed parts (or curtain-wall–to–punctures) always in favour of removed parts. The ratio between curtain/wall and punctures weakens the mass, showing the surface system that defines the volume.

Define the shell by using one building material only, treatment, or colour.

Show the thickness of the surface that defines the volume.

#thefastguidetoarchitecturalform

Architects Vesna and Matej Vozlič, *LINDE MPA*, Ljubljana, Slovenia.
photo by Blaž Budja

"Surfaces here are instead meeting-places, zones of encounter and admixture - the precise site that painting, cinema, architecture, fashion, or even the body all share, and where increasingly today they are transformed."

Giuliana Bruno

A VOLUME DEFINED BY A SERIES OF STAGGERED PLANES

 YOU CAN

Translate the planes of which the 'box' is made.
Divide the surface into several parts.
Crop the planes in irregular shapes.

YOU CAN'T

Close the 'box'.
Puncture the planes.

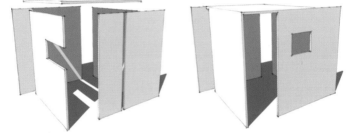

KEEP IN MIND

Define volume and spaces by bringing the surfaces near each other but without giving them any continuity: edges must not coincide.

Slide the surfaces a little just to expose the inside and outside. You can use different colours, building materials, and finishes.

Puncture between planes, misalignments, and edges, or mould the planes in different shapes.

#thefastguidetoarchitecturalform

Steven Holl Architects, *Planar House*, Paradise Valley, Arizona.
photo by © Jason Roehner

MVRDV, *Calveen Office Building*, Amersfoort, Netherlands.
photo by Rob 't Hart

FOLDING
#byfold

"Folding in Architecture was more or less my observation that architecture was becoming something defined by surfaces, not grids – a shift in the discipline from thinking of space in terms of coordinates, to space in terms of surfaces."

Greg Lynn

A VOLUME DEFINED BY ONE OR MORE FOLDED PLANES, PINPOINTING THE SUCCESSION OF INSIDE AND OUTSIDE

YOU CAN

Fold the planes in several directions.
Puncture them, but not much.
Use several planes.
Put different uses on top of each other.

YOU CAN'T

Break a plane's continuity.
Apply a set of punctures.
Use different building materials and/or colours on the planes.
Overlap the same layout in different conditions.

KEEP IN MIND

Insert curtain-walls between floors, but do not pass in front of folded planes.

Puncture curtain-walls that can be completely transparent, semitransparent, or opaque.

Do not puncture the continuous plane.

| #thefastguidetoarchitecturalform

Rem Koolhaas, *Educatorium*,
Utrecht, Netherlands.
photo by CAF

Fujiwara Muro Architects,
House in Muko, Kyoto, Japan.
photo by Toshiyuki Yano

"The visual data received by the eye is processed, manipulated, and filtered by the mind in its active search for structure and meaning."

Francis D. K. Ching

A VOLUME DEFINED BY A SEQUENCE OF CLOSE PLANES

YOU CAN

Translate and bend the planes.
Use planes of different sizes.

YOU CAN'T

Arrange the planes to be too distant from each other.
Puncture or cut the planes.

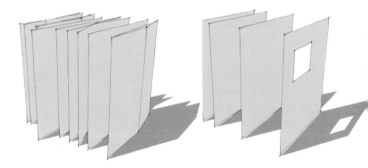

KEEP IN MIND

Bring vertical or horizontal planes close, not leaving much space between them. If needed, fold them and translate them slightly.

Insert transparent or opaque curtain-walls between the planes, so as to make the interruptions clear.

The planes must constitute the main structure of the building.

|

CAZA, *100 Walls Church*, Cebu City, Philippines.
photo by Iwan Baan. Copyright CAZA Architects.

Toyo Ito, *Tod's*, Tokyo, Japan.
photo by Res

"The form is cut off from its cause, from its method of original generation (classical or modernist vocabulary), and is reduced to a combination of data, which can be manipulated and processed ad infinitum."

Kengo Kuma

A VOLUME DEFINED BY WIREFRAME

YOU CAN

Fill the empty spaces.
Connect the empty spaces of the frame.
Let the design coincide with the structure.
Use even links.

YOU CAN'T

Add an independent set of punctures.
Arrange curtain-walls ahead of the wireframe.

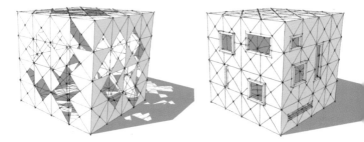

KEEP IN MIND

Follow a geometrical or parametric logic to draw the wireframe.

Use the wireframe as both facade and structure.

Place possible glass-walls or fillings in the empty spaces of the wireframe.

#thefastguidetoarchitecturalform

Heatherwick Studio, *UK Pavilion World Expo 2010*, Shanghai, China.
photo by Res

POINTFRAME
#pointframe

"An almost-nothing, wrapped around the object as a precious material that turns sharp and precise contours into blurry, opaque, and minimal."

Daniela Cerrocchi

A VOLUME DEFINED BY A DENSE ENSEMBLE OF PUNCTIFORM ELEMENTS

Apply sharp punctures in the pointframe
Slide the elements of the frame.
Cut big areas out of the pointframe.

Make the frame too thin.
Apply small punctures to the pointframe.

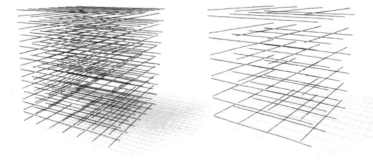

KEEP IN MIND

Pull together many punctiform elements, transparent or opaque (like optical fiber), leaving little space between them.

Remove parts of the volume (punctiform elements) and apply punctures in the excavations.

Use the space between punctiform elements, or the elements themselves, to let daylight in and to brighten the night.

SANAA, *Dior*, Tokyo, Japan.
photo by Res

DEMI-TRANSPARENCY
#trancesparency

"Goodness hides behind its gates
But even the President of the United States
Sometimes must have to stand naked."
Bob Dylan

VOLUMES DEFINED BY TRANSPARENT MATERIAL,
BRINGING THE LIGHT OUTSIDE FROM WITHIN AND VICE VERSA

YOU CAN

Alternate demi-transparency and total transparency.
Puncture.
Place opaque surfaces behind the shell in order to form a screen.
Study an independent set of punctures behind the transparent surface.

YOU CAN'T

Neglect obscuring and exposure.
Let the opaque surface prevail over the transparent one.

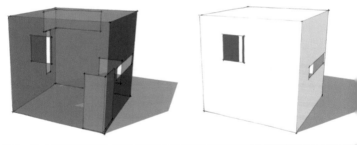

KEEP IN MIND

Crop the shell to insert transparent glass.

Screen the light by placing opaque panels behind the shell; think of the 'picture' that will be seen once lit inside.

Consider screening systems, energy saving, and maintenance.

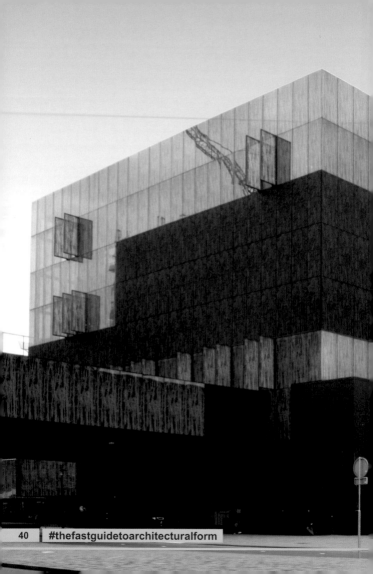

#thefastguidetoarchitecturalform

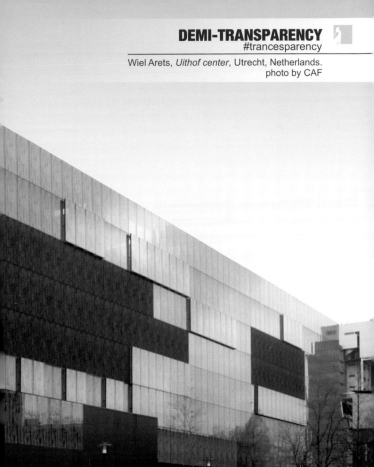

OPERATIONS ON VOLUME

"It's lack that gives us inspiration. It's not fullness."

Ray Bradbury

Amunt Architekten Martenson und Nagel Theissen, *JustK*, Tübingen, Germany.
photo by Brigida Gonzalez

"Poetry is a mirror which makes beautiful that which is distorted"

Percy Bysshe Shelley

A MOLDED VOLUME DRAWS ON THE ORIGINAL REGULAR SHAPE

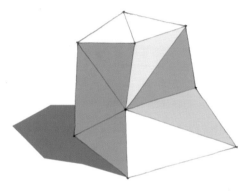

The resulting shape is the sum of one or more forces that, applied to a regular volume, mean to give it a new shape. The new shape will have to mind future uses, structures, and exposure.

KEEP IN MIND

Move and rotate edges and vertices of a regular solid and mould the shape while thinking of future uses.

Work on the starting volume without adding any matter.

Treat the whole surface evenly to underline it as one single volume.

#thefastguidetoarchitecturalform

de Architekten Cie., *the Whale*, Amsterdam, Netherlands.
photo by Res

Daniel Libeskind, *Jewish Museum*, Berlino, Germany.
photo by Guenter Schneider

OMA, *CCTV*, Beijing, China.
photo by Res

CLOSED FOLDING

"The most dangerous of all falsehoods is a slightly distorted truth."

Georg Christoph Lichtenberg

THE VOLUME PRESENTS ITSELF AS A FOLDED PARALLELEPIPED

This is a particular case of distortion where a parallelepiped is folded, mostly horizontally, forming it into a sort of pipe.

OPEN FOLDING

CLOSED FOLDING

KEEP IN MIND

Apply this distortion only when one of the three dimensions prevails over the others.

Fold once or more along the prevailing dimension.

Try to keep a constant section. Possible changes of section must either be aligned with the turns, or be gradual, in order to not create steps on the shell.

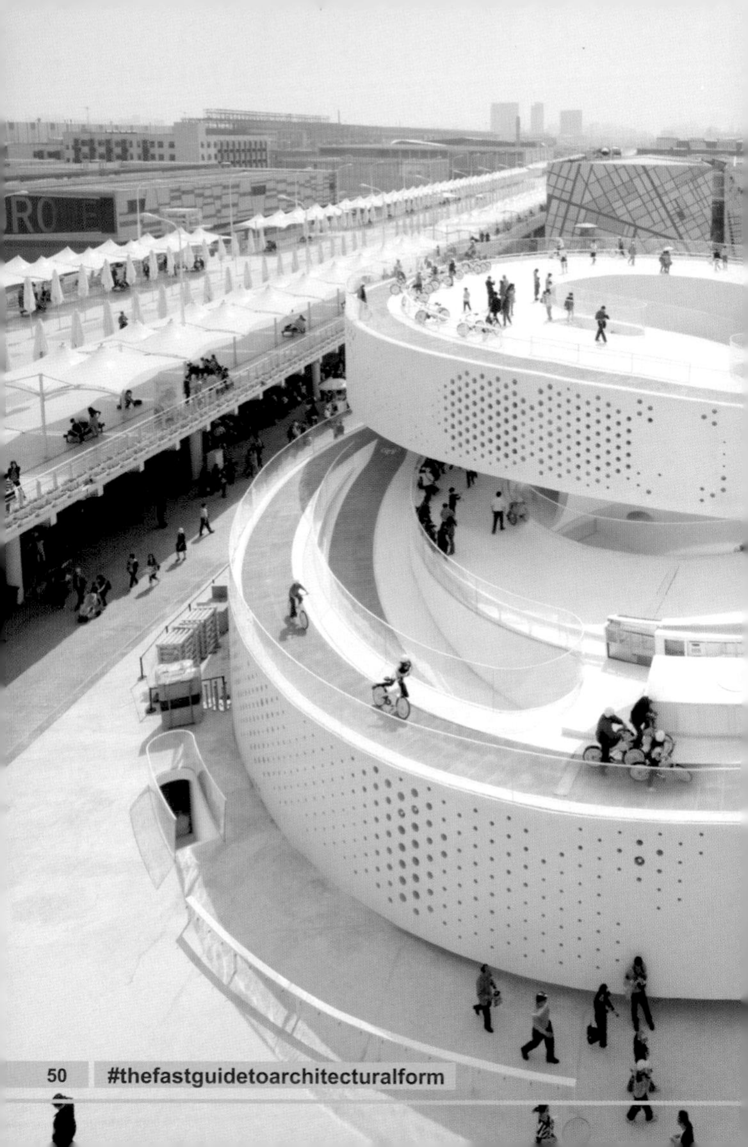
RO

3D FOLDING
#3distortion

BIG – Bjarke Ingels Group,
Denmark Pavilion, Expo Shanghai 2010, China.
photo by Iwan Baan

CLOSED FOLDING

Neutelings Riedijk, *IJ tower*, Amsterdam, Netherlands.
photo by David Bank

"Beauty: the adjustment of all parts proportionately so that one cannot add or subtract or change without impairing the harmony of the whole."

Leon Battista Alberti

VOLUME SEEMING TO HAVE BEEN CUT OUT AS IF MATTER HAD BEEN REMOVED FROM

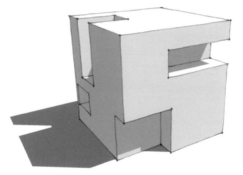

You must relate to the original shape to see the removal of matter from the volume.

Some buildings refer to time-eroded natural materials. In this case, if you soften the angles it will help you see the volume as a single excavated object.

KEEP IN MIND

Remove matter from the original volume, like you were cutting out and removing an insert.

Treat the surface of the original volume uniformly.

Use a different material or colour to treat the surface of the excavations (aligned with the removed parts) to make the whole operation easier to see.

53

dosmasuno arquitectos Ignacio Borrego, Néstor Montenegro and Lina Toro
Social services centre in móstoles, Madrid, Spain.
photo by, Miguel de Guzmán / ImagenSubliminal.com

TAKATO TAMAGAMI ARCHITECTURAL DESIGN and
Be-Fun DESIGN H-studio, *SUNWELL MUSE Kitasando,* Tokyo, Japan.
Image © Masaya Yoshimura

"Manufacturing is more than just putting parts together. It's coming up with ideas, testing principles and perfecting the engineering, as well as final assembly."

James Dyson

THE VOLUME IS CUT INTO TWO OR MORE PARTS

The cropped parts can be slightly translated and/or rotated, or they can be put together again to form one single volume where the removed part is replaced by another material, usually transparent.

Separation with curved cropping surfaces and translated parts.

KEEP IN MIND

Divide original volume into two or more parts, thinking of the uses and spaces that will result.

Use the same material in every part to show the original volume. You can use another material, but only in the part of the facade correspondent with the cut.

Do not leave too much space between the separated parts and, if needed, rotate and/or translate slightly.

tguidetoarchitecturalform

SUPPOSE DESIGN OFFICE
House in Usita Shinmachi, Hiroshima, Japan.
photo by Toshiyuki Yano

Herzog & De Meuron, *1111 Lincoln Road*, Miami, Florida.
Andrew Wall Photography

"Looking for a great teacher who can tell you what will happen in the future? Ask the ancient ruins what will happen!"

Mehmet Murat ildan

THE VOLUME SEEMING UNFINISHED

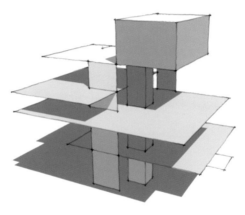

The shape is the sum of basic building and structural elements, distorted and leaving many empty spaces to stress the idea of 'unfinished'.

KEEP IN MIND

Mould your volume using structural elements, such as floors, beams, walls, and pillars.

Distort the structural elements to make the structure formally heterogeneous.

Add balustrades, curtain-walls, and punctures, with as little visible as possible and without the filled parts ever prevailing on the empty ones.

Ensamble Studio, *Hemeroscopium House*, Las Rozas, Madrid, Spain.
photo Courtesy of Ensamble Studio

Studio Fuksas, *Admirant Entrance Building*, Eindhoven, Netherlands.
photo © Moreno Maggi

HYPERSHAPE/ABSTRACTION

#ipershape

"There is no abstract art. You must always start with something.
Afterward you can remove all traces of reality."

Pablo Picasso

A VOLUME CONFIGURED AS AN ORGANIC MASS

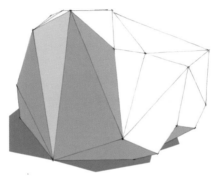

Parametrically controlled shapes prove to be abstract or organic, and they answer to geometries belonging to a higher level that in no way can be reduced to the original solid.

KEEP IN MIND

Deny Euclidean geometry and Platonic solids, use only higher-level geometries.

Use computer software to simulate organic shapes; you must be able to control the shape parametrically, in order to make the volumes easily feasible.

Designate one material only to the volume. If the shell does not coincide with the structural system, apply punctures independently.

#thefastguidetoarchitecturalform

Peter Cook and Colin Fournier, *Kunsthaus Graz,* Austria.
photo by Marion Schneider & Christoph Aistleitner

OPERATIONS AMONG VOLUMES

"The composition is the organized sum of the interior functions of every part of the work."

Wassily Kandinsky

EIFFEL TOWER

Paris, France.
photo by Wladyslaw

EIFFEL TOWER

Burj Khalifa - Dubai

Canton Tower - Guangzhou

CN Tower - Toronto

Petronas Twin - Kuala Lumpur

Empire State Building New York

"Fashion is architecture: it is a matter of proportions."
Coco Chanel

THE SCALE AND PROPORTION OF SHAPES ARE POINTLESS IDEAS UNLESS RELATED WITH OTHER VOLUMES

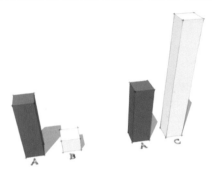

Volume **A** is both tall, if compared with volume **B**, and short, if compared with volume **C**. The proportion of volumes **A** and **C** configure them as slender.

Size is made of physical dimensions conveyed by length, width, and depth. At the same time these dimensions determine the proportions of the shape, the scale is determined by its dimensions compared with other shapes in the same context.

KEEP IN MIND

If you want a volume to look tall, put it near a short one. If you want it to look short, put it near a tall one.

If you want to fling the building in one direction, the size of the volume in that direction must be much bigger than in the others.

Use contrast to underline dimensional, chromatic, or aesthetic traits.

JOINT BY SLIDING

"When I design buildings, I think of the overall composition, much as the parts of a body would fit together. On top of that, I think about how people will approach the building and experience that space."

Tadao Ando

SHAPE IS CONFIGURED AS THE RESULT
OF THE JOINING OF TWO OR MORE VOLUMES

JOINT BY SLIDING

**JOINT BETWEEN VOLUMES
OF DIFFERENT HEIGHT**

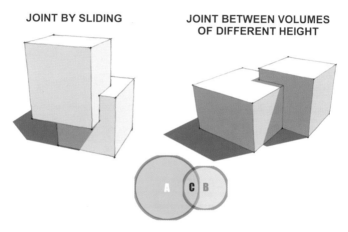

Joint is a particular type of mutual relationship between volumes were the part of intersection is space in common (**C**).

KEEP IN MIND

Always show the joint by sliding the volumes and working on sizes to diversify them by height and depth; the faces of the joined volumes must never be placed on the same plane.

Keep in mind that the joint between two volumes generates a third space that is, at the same time, part of the first and the second volume. Give this space a particular purpose and/or use.

You can, if you like, treat the two volumes in a different manner.

73

#thefastguidetoarchitecturalform

Studio Libeskind, *Royal Ontario Museum*, Toronto, Canada.
photo by Tony Hisgett

**JOINT BETWEEN VOLUMES
OF DIFFERENT HEIGHT**

dosmasuno arquitectos, *Carabanchel Housing*, Madrid, Spain.
photo © Miguel de Guzmán / ImagenSubliminal.com

EXCAVATION

"Anyone who has become entranced by the sound of water drops in the darkness of a ruin can attest to the extraordinary capacity of the ear to carve a volume into the void of darkness. The space traced by the ear becomes a cavity sculpted in the interior of the mind."

Steven Holl

THE ADDITION OF A VOLUME AS SUPERFETATION OF MASS; ADDITION OF VOLUME THAT SIMULATES A MASS SUBTRACTION

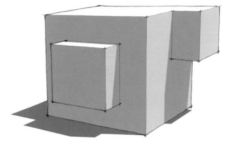

SUPERFETATION: a particular kind of addition in which one volume is attached to another one. The volumes do not share any areas, but they are in continuity (next to one another, without joints).

EXCAVATION: a particular kind of addition in which the parts making the volume help show the whole system as a single eroded volume.

KEEP IN MIND

Locate the matrix volume of the project and put smaller volumes horizontally close to it in order to leave both volumes clearly visible.

Treat every part with the same material if you want the volume to appear as a single excavated one. Normally, systems of punctures on projecting and receding parts are independent and diversified between them.

Use different materials and different systems of punctures if you want the close volumes to appear as superfetations on the matrix volume.

#thefastguidetoarchitecturalform

MVRDV, WoZoCo, Amsterdam, Netherlands.
photo by Rob 't Hart

SUPERFETATION

SANAA, *VNew Art Museum,* New York.
photo by Nick-D

"Repetition bestows on the building an ideal motor organ that with its throbbing, gives a biological temporality, a cadence of beats and intervals"

Franco Purini

VOLUMES PUT CLOSE TO EACH OTHER
AND REPEATED BY ADHERENCE (NO INTERSECTION)

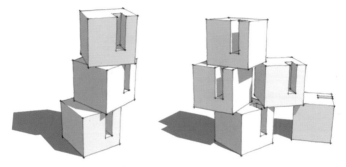

Overlapped volumes (**A-B**) might be of the same shape, material and treatment, but they can also be treated differently or be of different shapes.

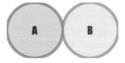

KEEP IN MIND

Overlap volumes whose shapes can be easily distinguished, careful not to entangle them.

Rotate and/or slide a little to pull out, or put back in, one volume with respect to the volumes it leans on.

Treat the volumes as you see fit, using the colours, materials, and finishing of your choice, puncturing according to the rules described in this text.

#thefastguidetoarchitecturalform

James Stewart Polshek, *Rose Center for Earth and Space*, New York.
photo by Alfred Gracombe

INCLUSION
#inclusaction

"It's not exclusive, but inclusive, which is the whole spirit of jazz."

Herbie Hancock

A VOLUME INCLUDED IN ANOTHER VOLUME

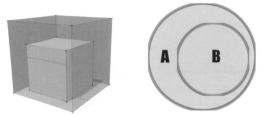

The inclusion of a volume in another one transforms the space of the containing volume, creating two different spaces organized in a hierarchy: one (**A**) between the two volumes and one inside the contained volume (**B**).

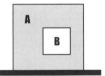

A space around volume
B volume inside container

KEEP IN MIND

Remember to leave an empty space between the container and the contained volume, big enough to make both volumes clearly recognizable.

Make the space between the two volumes (container and contained) usable on every side. Should the included volume be suspended, arrange the spaces above and below it.

Use pure shapes for the container volume in order to make the contained volume more recognizable.

85

INCLUSION
#inclusaction

Oving Architekten, *Overkapping commandantswoning*,
Westerbork, Netherlands.
photo by Susan Schuls

Steven Holl Architects, *Nelson Atkins Museum*, Kansas City, Missouri.
photo by Marc Teer

UNDERGROUND LINK

Steven Holl Architects, *Linked Hybrid*, Beijing, China.
photo by Res

AIR LINK

*"The weakest link in the chain is also the strongest.
It can break the chain."*

Stanislaw Jerzy Lec

**FORMAL SYSTEMS MADE OF SEVERAL VOLUMES ARE
VISUALLY PERMEABLE. BUT THEY CAN BE PHYSICALLY LINKED.**

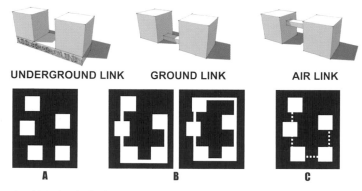

UNDERGROUND LINK   **GROUND LINK**   **AIR LINK**

A   **B**   **C**

A - Not physically linking the volumes or linking them underground means you are not connecting them visually.

B - The ground link separates open public space up to the point it becomes private, in which case the link is closed in a ring. pp. 90-91

C - Connecting volumes with air links means leaving the public space untouched, but connecting the volumes visually.

KEEP IN MIND

Physically link several volumes with a ground passage if you want the formal system to present itself as a barrier.

If you do not physically connect the volumes, keep in mind that the open space will carry out this job and will have to be designed accordingly. In the case of underground volume links, think about possible systems/excavations that will allow air and light in the buried part.

Use air links to connect volumes both visually and physically, not touching the existing spatial continuity on the ground.

CONTAINER DESIGN / Takanobu Kishimoto,
House of awa-cho, Tokushima-shi, Japan
photo by Eiji Tomita

GROUND LINK

MVRDV, *Frøsilos*, Copenhagen, Denmark.
photo by Rob 't Hart

ONE PREDOMINANT DIRECTION

DIRECTIONS

#buildirection

*"Directions are instructions given to explain how.
Direction is a vision offered to explain why."*

Simon Sinek

CENTRIC SHAPES ARE STATIC.
DIRECTIONAL SHAPES ENCOURAGE MOVEMENT

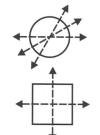

UNLIMITED PREDOMINANT DIRECTIONS
SPHERE/CYLINDER/CONE (circular base)
Omnidirectional centric system

TWO PREDOMINANT DIRECTIONS
PARALLELEPIPED (square base)
Bidirectional centric system

ONE PREDOMINANT DIRECTION
DOUBLE SPHERE/CYLINDER/CONE
Linear system

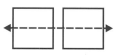

ONE PREDOMINANT DIRECTION
DOUBLE CUBE
Linear system

KEEP IN MIND

If you want the volume to be seen in the same way when approached from any direction, use a cylindrical shape and treat it with one material only.

If you want the volume to be seen in the same way when approached from two orthogonal directions, use a square shape.

If you want the volume to have one predominant direction, use a parallelepiped or, as an alternative, a series of volumes along a straight line and close to each other.

#thefastguidetoarchitecturalform

SANAA, *21st Century Museum of Contemporary Art*, Kanazawa, Japan
photo by open image data of kanazawa city

UNLIMITED PREDOMINANT DIRECTIONS

"I know that the twelve notes in each octave and the variety of rhythm offer me opportunities that all of human genius will never exhaust."

Igor Stravinsky

A REPEATED VOLUME MEASURES THE SPACE SHOWING ITSELF AS PART OF A SINGLE SYSTEM

LINEAR SERIES

PLANAR SERIES

A series is the repetition of a single element at regular intervals along an axis or a plane. To present itself as a series, the repeated element must be ascribable either by equivalence or simile (material or formal) to the other elements composing the series.

The series can also be developed on links set at regular intervals, but in this case the repeated element must always be the same.

Remember that, normally, the opening and the closing volume of a series (**A–Z**) form an exception, and they present themselves as origin and conclusion of the set by changes of shape and/or treatment.

KEEP IN MIND

Use the same shapes and/or treatments to make all the volumes in the series ascribable to one single system.

Arrange the volumes along an axis or as links, always leaving the same amount of empty space between them. The interval in the repetition introduces the idea of rhythm so the series can be recognized and measured.

If you develop the series at irregular intervals, use the same elements or you'll only obtain a list of disconnected volumes.

#thefastguidetoarchitecturalform

MVRDV, *Didden Village*, Rotterdam, Netherlands.
photo by Rob 't Hart

EXCEPTION BY POSITION and TREATMENT

Guedes Cruz Architects, *Social Complex*, Alcabideche, Portugal.
photo by Ricardo Oliveira Alves

EXCEPTION BY SHAPE

"The two elements the traveler first captures in the big city are extra human architecture and furious rhythm. Geometry and anguish."

Federico Garcia Lorca

EXCEPTION MAKES SERIALITY STRONGER

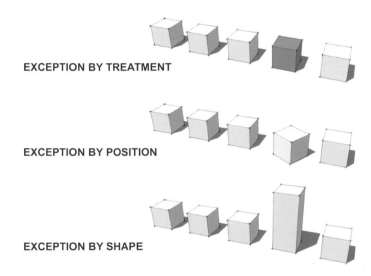

EXCEPTION BY TREATMENT

EXCEPTION BY POSITION

EXCEPTION BY SHAPE

KEEP IN MIND

Make sure the matrix series is made of enough repeated elements to be clearly understandable before inserting the exceptions.

Insert exceptional elements (by shape, position, colour, and material) to emphasize the idea of the series.

Insert the exceptions by skipping one or more elements of the series. Place the exception in that empty space as you like. Remember that the 'gap', too, can be considered as an exception.

#thefastguidetoarchitecturalform

Uchida Takahisa Architect Design Office,
T-NURSERY, Fukuoka, Japan.
photo by Hiroyuki Kawano

EXCEPTION BY TREATMENT

GROUND CONNECTION

"Architecture is bound to situation, and I feel like the site is a metaphysical link, a poetic link, to what a building can be."

Steven Holl

Josep Miàs, market, Barcellona, pp. 108-109 **5**

Renzo Piano, Richard Rogers, *Centre Pompidou*, Paris, pp. 114-115 **6**

Jean Nouvel, *Institut du monde arabe*, Paris **7**

"Each city receives its shape from the desert it opposes."

Italo Calvino

THE POSITION OF THE VOLUME CONFIGURES THE SPACE

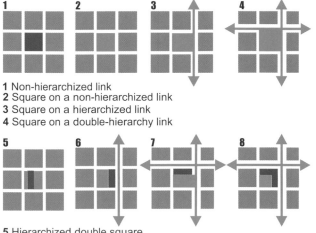

1 Non-hierarchized link
2 Square on a non-hierarchized link
3 Square on a hierarchized link
4 Square on a double-hierarchy link

5 Hierarchized double square
6 Indrawn square
7 Extrovert square
8 Double-indrawn square

KEEP IN MIND

Define the square by placing the volumes that contain it or, alternatively, place the volume to create a well-defined open space.

Use the size of the empty space and the height of the volumes defining the square to make it proportionate.

Place the volume in the middle of the empty space if you want to create two different areas.

|

SHAPE AND OPEN SPACE
#voidshape

Josep Miàs, *market*, Barcellona, Spain.
photo by BrrE

HIERARCHIZED DOUBLE SQUARE

Barrier with the longest faces open
SANAA, *Summer Pavilion 2009, Serpentine Gallery,*
Kensington Gardens London.
photo by Cjc13

Barrier with longitudinal face open
René van Zuuk Architekten, *ARCAM,* Amsterdam, Netherlands.
photo by Res

"Urban buildings are often shapers of space"
Matthew Frederick

THE SHAPE CREATES PASSAGES AND OPENINGS

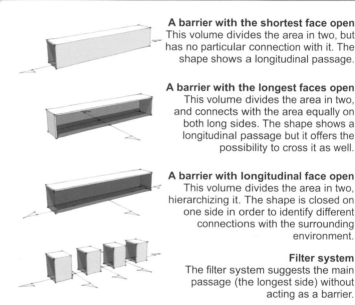

A barrier with the shortest face open
This volume divides the area in two, but has no particular connection with it. The shape shows a longitudinal passage.

A barrier with the longest faces open
This volume divides the area in two, and connects with the area equally on both long sides. The shape shows a longitudinal passage but it offers the possibility to cross it as well.

A barrier with longitudinal face open
This volume divides the area in two, hierarchizing it. The shape is closed on one side in order to identify different connections with the surrounding environment.

Filter system
The filter system suggests the main passage (the longest side) without acting as a barrier.

KEEP IN MIND

Use shape and the treatment of the prospects to show openings and closures, front and rear.

Arrange the volume longitudinally to separate spaces with different functions or purposes.

Use architectural systems made of several elements to preserve physical permeability but which give directions on passages and resting places.

#thefastguidetoarchitecturalform

Renzo Piano, Richard Rogers,
Centro Georges Pompidou, Paris, France.
photo by BIBI

LAID
#lieground

"Beyond place and action and given time/and love's labours/the glove had already set down in that never-ending painting/where Psyche and Cupid rule together/where Psyche and Cupid smile together"

Francesco De Gregori

A LAID VOLUME DIVIDES THE SPACE PHYSICALLY

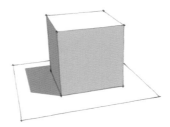

The volume separates the **A-B** space.
Around the volume, qualities and features of the space do not change.

KEEP IN MIND

Lay the volume down to separate an area, both physically and visually.

Use the shape to suggest directions and passages, respecting the already existing ones.

Expose the entrance of the architectural system.

#thefastguidetoarchitecturalform

Alberto Campo Baeza, *Moliner House*, Zaragoza, Spain
photo by Javier Callejas

JHK Architecten, *deBrug / deKade*, Rotterdam, Netherlands.
photo by Res

JagerJanssen architects + DREISSEN architects,
Restaurant Het Bosch, Amsterdam, Netherlands.
photo by John Lewis Marshall

"He who would learn to fly one day must first learn to stand and walk and run and climb and dance; one cannot fly into flying."

Friedrich Nietzsche

A SUSPENDED VOLUME MAINTAINES GROUND CONTINUITY, IDENTIFYING A COVERED OPEN SPACE

The volume identifies two types of space, **A-A1**.
The features of space **A** do not change, while space **A1**, although in continuity with space **A**, has different features.

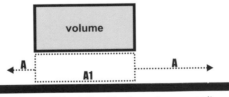

Space **A1** is defined by the volume over it.

KEEP IN MIND

Lift the volume from the ground if you do not want to alter the continuity of the open space.

The space on the ground must have a fluid and non-hierarchized passageway. Possible hierarchies must be identified by treatment of the soil.

Assign different functions to the open space, separating the space 'under' the volume from the one beyond it.

#thefastguidetoarchitecturalform

Delugan Meissl, *Porsche Museum*, Stuttgart, Germany.
photo by Rick Ligthelm / flirck.com

deca ARCHITECTURE, *Aloni*, Antiparos, Greece.
Photograph courtesy of **deca**ARCHITECTURE

"The land is the only thing in the world worth working for, worth fighting for, worth dying for, because it's the only thing that lasts."

Gerald O'Hara (Gone With The Wind)

**THE VOLUME EMBEDDED IN THE GROUND DOES NOT VISUALLY CHANGE THE EXISTING LANDSCAPE.
IT COULD IDENTIFY OPEN SPACES BELOW GROUND LEVEL.**

The landscape apparently doesn't change, although the excavation divides it in two parts **A** and **C**.
The volume identifies a new space **B**.
Spaces **A** and **C** have features that are unchanged.
Space **B** is born.
Space **B** is deeper and is delimited by the sides of the excavation.

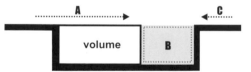

Space **B** is deeper and is delimited by the sides of the excavation

KEEP IN MIND

Bury the volume if you want to conceal it in the landscape and create a soft approach with the surrounding landscape.

Consider at least one pertinent area below the ground to allow air and light in the building.

Signal the architectural system planning spaces and volumetric elements above ground.

#thefastguidetoarchitecturalform

BIG – Bjarke Ingels Group,
Danish National Maritime Museum, Helsingor, Denmark
photo by Luca Santiago Mora

FINAL FIREWORKS
complexity is more

#wyreframe
#buildsubtraction
#seriexception
#lieground

Atelier Deshaus, *Kindergarten of Jiading New Town*, Shanghai, China.
photo by Shu He

#massmatter
#trancesparency
#3distortion
#buildsubtraction
#separaction
#lieground

TRULY FAKE

80% of issues in Architecture is fixed by "rotate and mirror".
(Elio Ravà)

Architecture is frontier-art. Only if you accept the challenge of contamination it has a reason to exist. Otherwise is armchair stuff. (Renzo Piano)

Architecture is too important to be given to architects.
(Giancarlo De Carlo)

A good solution in Architecture always points at the problem where it came from. Its problem, its reason for being. (Giorgio Grassi)

Apartment: a box that is placed in a bigger box that is placed in a packed place called block . (Giancarlo Tramutoli)

Architecture is the art of how to waste space. (Philip Johnson)

We shape our buildings; thereafter they shape us.
(Winston Churchill)

Architecture is the learned game, correct and magnificent, of forms assembled in the light. (Le Corbusier)

Architecture is a visual art, and the buildings speak for themselves.
(Julia Morgan)

Every great architect is - necessarily - a great poet. He must be a great original interpreter of his time, his day, his age.
(Frank Lloyd Wright)

Good buildings come from good people, and all problems are solved by good design. (Stephen Gardiner)

Architecture is the reaching out for the truth. (Louis Kahn)

A house is a machine for living in. (Le Corbusier)

Architecture is basically a container of something. I hope they will enjoy not so much the teacup, but the tea. (Yoshio Taniguchi)

I call architecture frozen music. (Johann Wolfgang von Goethe)

Form follows profit is the aesthetic principle of our times.
(Richard Rogers)

#thefastguidetoarchitecturalform

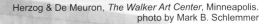

Herzog & De Meuron, *The Walker Art Center*, Minneapolis.
photo by Mark B. Schlemmer

#massmatter
#trancesparency
#twistortion
#buildsubtraction
#incastraction
#lieground
#buildrone

TRULY FAKE

Architecture is invention. (Oscar Niemeyer)

Each new situation requires a new architecture. (Jean Nouvel)

Nothing requires the architect's care more than the due proportions of buildings. (Vitruvius)

My work is not about 'form follows function,' but 'form follows beauty' or, even better, 'form follows feminine.' (Oscar Niemeyer)

Form follows beauty. (Oscar Niemeyer)

Fashion should be a form of escapism, and not a form of imprisonment. (Alexander McQueen)

Every form is a base for colour, every colour is the attribute of a form. (Victor Vasarely)

Buildings are forms of performances. (Rafael Vinoly)

Form follows function - that has been misunderstood. Form and function should be one, joined in a spiritual union. (Frank Lloyd Wright)

It would follow that 'significant form' was form behind which we catch a sense of ultimate reality. (Clive Bell)

Buildings should serve people, not the other way around. (John Portman)

They can do without architecture who have no olives nor wines in the cellar. (Henry David Thoreau)

Every building is a prototype. No two are alike. (Helmut Jahn)

What people want, above all, is order. (Stephen Gardiner)

Don't clap too hard - it's a very old building. (John Osborne)

Not many architects have the luxury to reject significant things. (Rem Koolhaas)

There are no rules of architecture for a castle in the clouds. (Gilbert K. Chesterton)

MVRDV, *Expo 2000 Netherlands Pavilion*, Hanover, Germany.
photo by Rob 't Hart

#massmatter #trancesparency #buildsubtraction
#incompletaction #inclusaction #buildrone

Steven Holl, *Loisium Hotel*, Langenlois, Austria.
photo by Hamster28

#massmatter
#twistortion
#buildsubtraction
#lieground

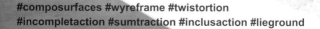

#composurfaces #wyreframe #twistortion
#incompletaction #sumtraction #inclusaction #lieground

heri&salli, *Office Off*, Burgenland, Austria
photo by © Paul Ott

ACKNOWLEDGMENTS

To **Elio Ravá**: I thank you because this research was born from your idea to transform everything we have been telling our students for years into a book, finally giving a scientific status to a subject that didn't really have it before. I thank you also for following me, putting up with me and helping me to correct, shape, and finish this book, and my PhD dissertation as well (which this book is a part of).

To **Silvia Antonini**: I thank you for the enthusiasm and willingness that you have put into translating everything that had to be translated—these lines as well. I thank you also for helping me keeping the contacts with all the firms that have kindly allowed me to use the pictures that are in the book and for the practical and moral support during the complicated part of defining the text.

To **all the Students**: I am thanking all of you, because reviewing your works has helped me to clarify and sort all the contents that have now become this book. I had to make it clear first to myself so I could afterwards explain to you how to 'perform operations' on the shapes of buildings. And I'd like to remind you that this kind of operation comes long after many others.

Rudolf van Wezel: I thank you for the patience and the advice that you have given me since I first sent you the draft of this book. Thank you for your trusting me first, and shaping these pages after.

#thefastguidetoarchitecturalform

Rem Koolhaas, *Central Library,* Seattle, Washington.
photo by Bobak Ha'Eri

#wyreframe
#trancesparency
#twistortion
#lieground

#massmatter
#trancesparency
#buildsubtraction
#lieground

BIOGRAPHY

Baires Raffaelli (1975) graduated *cum laude* in Architecture at Rome La Sapienza University, where he has been researching and teaching for years in the field of Architecture Planning and Design to both Architecture and Engineering students.

He has PhD in Architecture, Theory and Planning. Baires Raffaelli has performed research within the fields of housing, population density, and public spaces. The results of this research have been widely discussed and studied, and they have also been the source for partnerships among universities, public authority, and private companies.

He is a co-founder of BRRE Architects, and with this firm he has received both national and international rewards.

His projects and research have often been subjects of articles in architecture magazines.